What Every Teacher Should Know About Creating Digital Teaching Portfolios

Clare R. Kilbane
University of Massachusetts at Amherst

Natalie B. Milman
The George Washington University

Boston   New York   San Francisco
Mexico City   Montreal   Toronto   London   Madrid   Munich   Paris
Hong Kong   Singapore   Tokyo   Cape Town   Sydney

WHAT EVERY TEACHER SHOULD KNOW ABOUT CREATING DIGITAL TEACHING PORTFOLIOS

Clare R. Kilbane & Natalie B. Milman

TABLE OF CONTENTS

CHAPTER 1: PORTFOLIOS, TEACHING PORTFOLIOS, AND DIGITAL TEACHING PORTFOLIOS

CHAPTER 2: SOME BENEFITS OF DIGITAL TEACHING PORTFOLIOS

CHAPTER 3: THE DIGITAL TEACHING PORTFOLIO PROCESS

Table of Contents from **Kilbane, C.R., & Milman, N.B. (2003).** *The Digital Teaching Portfolio Handbook: A How-to Guide for Educators.* Boston: Allyn & Bacon.

What Every Teacher Should Know About Creating Digital Teaching Portfolios

CHAPTER 1: PORTFOLIOS, TEACHING PORTFOLIOS, AND DIGITAL TEACHING PORTFOLIOS

What is a portfolio?

A portfolio is a goal-driven, organized, collection of materials that demonstrates a person's expansion of knowledge and skills over time. The contents, organization, and presentation of materials in portfolios vary greatly depending on their audience and purpose. However, all portfolios display tangible evidence of an individual's growth and development.

What are professional portfolios?

Professional portfolios might be described as purposeful compilations of and reflections on a professional's work, effort, and progress in her or his field. Portfolios are used in various professions, including architecture, the arts, and education. Professional portfolios, in their most basic form, are documentation tools that capture vivid "snapshots" of critical moments in a professional's growth. Portfolios illustrate these moments through various physical artifacts or professional materials.

There are two types of professional portfolios—working portfolios and presentation portfolios. These types of portfolios have different purposes and audiences.

What are working portfolios?

Working portfolios are generally large, complete compilations of a person's work over a certain time period. Working portfolios may contain examples of a professional's work throughout her or his entire career or encompass a shorter time period. Working portfolios are stored in many different containers including fancy leather notebooks, large canvas bags, boxes, milk cartons, folders, computer hard drives, disks, or even CD's. Regardless of their physical size and shape, working portfolios store a vast array of artifacts that demonstrate an individual's strengths and weaknesses in her or his professional work. Working portfolios are often used in conjunction with a presentation portfolio.

What is a presentation portfolio?

A presentation portfolio includes a subset of the items found in a working portfolio. Materials are selected as representative pieces from the working portfolio for a variety of reasons and each is deliberately chosen after personal reflection. Various criteria are used in selecting materials for inclusion in a presentation portfolio. In some cases, materials are selected to reflect specific goals or a set of standards. In these cases, the portfolio might be considered an "evaluative portfolio"-meaning that professionals can be evaluated with this portfolio. Professional groups in a variety of fields have developed standards that are being used as guidelines for the presentation and evaluation of portfolios.

In other instances, a portfolio might be created for a specific audience or a group of individuals who are interviewing the portfolio creator for a job. Portfolios used for this purpose are often called "employment portfolios." To learn about the different types of presentation portfolios that exist, read Chapter 1, "Portfolios, Teaching Portfolios, and Digital Teaching Portfolios," of Kilbane, C.R., & Milman, N.B. (2003). *The Digital Teaching Portfolio Handbook: A How-to Guide for Educators*. Boston: Allyn & Bacon.

2

What is a Teaching Portfolio?

A teaching portfolio is a special type of presentation portfolio that demonstrates the professional competence of anyone who engages in the act of teaching. Teaching portfolios are created by teachers who work with students at the elementary school, middle school, high school, and university level. Although more widespread use of portfolios occurs at the k-12 levels, portfolios for college instructors are becoming more popular. Many institutions of higher education across the country are beginning to use portfolios during tenure and merit review processes.

Teaching portfolios contain a variety of materials or artifacts from teaching. These materials include curriculum units, course syllabi, notes to parents and/or students (i.e., email, newsletters, etc.), student writing samples, photographs from teaching environments, and videos of classroom interactions. They also may include letters of recommendation, records of academic work, and teaching evaluations. Although a teaching portfolio does indeed teach those viewing it about the creator's professional competence, its name is derived from the type of work it displays rather than the instructional work it performs.

Teaching portfolios have several critical attributes. According to Lee Shulman (1998), President of the Carnegie Foundation for the Advancement of Teaching, a teaching portfolio is a "structured documentary history of a set of coached or mentored acts of teaching, substantiated by samples of student portfolios, and fully realized only through reflective writing, deliberation, and conversation" (p. 37). The deliberate selection, reflection, and communication revolving around the materials included in a true teaching portfolio distinguish it from other types of portfolios that might be used to organize information for employment or other such purposes.

What are Digital Teaching Portfolios?

Digital teaching portfolios, sometimes referred to as multimedia portfolios, electronic portfolios, e-folios, webfolios and electronically-augmented portfolios, contain the same content traditional teaching portfolios include but present these professional materials in digital format. In digital teaching portfolios, professional materials related to the teaching process, or artifacts, are presented using a combination of multimedia technologies. Teaching portfolios often include audiorecordings, hypermedia programs, databases, spreadsheets, video, and web pages. Such portfolios are stored on disks, CD's, zip disks, or file servers accessible through the World Wide Web.

In the future, if dreams of "paperless offices," and workplaces where most written communication occurs in digital format become a reality, it may not be necessary to call portfolios produced digitally "digital teaching portfolios." But until then, we will use this phrase to distinguish them from "traditional portfolios" that present "hard copies" of professional materials on paper in binders or other containers.

Advantages of Digital Teaching Portfolios

There are several advantages to presenting teaching portfolios in digital format. Some result from the process of creating portfolios this way and others result from the product of the digital portfolio. Here we present a brief list:

1. Digital technology facilitates the reproduction of portfolio content:

Several factors related to traditional portfolios make it a good idea to reproduce portfolio content in digital format. First, traditional portfolios contain precious, often irreplaceable material. If this material is digitized, original copies of artifacts can be protected and the digital version can be circulated instead. Second, traditional portfolios are often heavy and awkward to carry--sometimes requiring special bags for transportation. Once materials are converted to digital format, a portfolio's contents become as compact as the storage medium on which it resides (i.e. CD-ROM, Zip disk, etc).

2. Digital teaching portfolios are easy and inexpensive to duplicate:

Teachers who invest the time and energy in creating a portfolio do so because they want to share their work with others. But traditional portfolios are often so large and their contents can be so valuable that one copy of a portfolio is not enough to meet a teacher's desire to share it. Reproducing traditional portfolios in paper format using photocopiers is an option. But, duplication of traditional portfolio contents in this way is expensive when artifacts are multi-colored, and complicated when they are different sizes and shapes. Once materials are digitized in the process of creating a digital teaching portfolio, multiple copies of a portfolio can be made easily for little additional expense. The same process used to create the first copy of a digital portfolio can be repeated to create myriad duplicates. CD ROMs bought in bulk often cost less than $.05 a piece and webspace can be inexpensive or free.

3. Digital teaching portfolios support greater creativity:

Digital production techniques support non-linear design and the seamless integration of various media formats. Teachers who know how to maximize multimedia formats can better demonstrate their ability to design effective instructional materials in this medium than in more traditional ones. If they know how, teachers can blend various sensory stimuli to communicate their ideas and skills more effectively and in more engaging ways in digital teaching portfolios.

4. Digital teaching portfolios can communicate a teacher's competence in using technology:

Digital teaching portfolios are one of the best ways for teachers to communicate the level of their knowledge and skill with educational technologies. The increasing role of technology in learning environments makes the demonstration of technology competence more important now than ever before. Teachers who create portfolios in this way demonstrate their knowledge of hardware, software, and the integration of the two for the purpose of creating useful educational tools.

5. Creating DTPs can act as catalysts for teachers' professional development:

The process of creating a digital teaching portfolio can benefit a teacher's professional development even more than the act of creating a traditional teaching portfolio. Although the process of making traditional teaching portfolios helps teachers examine their competence and chart their future growth as professionals, the creation of digital teaching portfolios also provides them the opportunity to think more seriously about how their career will be affected by the role of technology in the classroom and society.

6. Digital teaching portfolios can be used to build community:

The low-costs and ease associated with sharing digital teaching portfolios allow them to be made available inexpensively or free to large numbers of people. In this way, the contents of

6

digital teaching portfolios can be easily shared with the members of the local and global community. Such information sharing can build support for teachers' efforts while promoting teacher excellence and professionalism.

Challenges Associated With Digital Teaching Portfolios

Although there are advantages to creating portfolios in digital format, some challenges arise when this format is chosen over more traditional ones. Here we elaborate on just a few.

1. The creation of digital teaching portfolios requires a great level of knowledge and a wider variety of skills:

Even though the creation of a traditional teaching portfolio requires a teacher to possess significant professional knowledge, digital teaching portfolios require even more knowledge and skill. To create a teaching portfolio in digital format, teachers must not only have knowledge about portfolios in general, but also about digital portfolios in particular. In addition, they must be able to use various types of hardware and software and integrate various multimedia materials in an organized, visually pleasing package. When teachers do not possess this expertise, they are unable to share their competence in this format and unable to benefit from them.

2. The creation of digital teaching portfolios requires professional support:

Teachers need good teachers if they are going to learn how to create their own digital teaching portfolios. But more often than not, school districts lack the professional development personnel required to aid teachers with the development of digital portfolios.

3. Creating digital teaching portfolios requires expensive equipment:

Even though the materials a teacher needs to create a traditional teaching portfolio (including paper, binders, felt, ribbons, photographs, index cards, etc.) cost money, few are as expensive as those required to create a digital teaching portfolio. High-tech equipment comes with an equally high price tag. In addition, it is usually expensive to repair when it breaks down and quickly becomes obsolete.

4. Creating digital teaching portfolios requires more time and energy:

Although the time invested in creating a digital teaching portfolio yields many rewards, it still requires more than producing a portfolio in traditional format. Additional time spent learning how to use hardware and software can be too time consuming, especially for teachers with limited technology skills.

5. Viewing digital teaching portfolios requires viewers have technical skills and powerful, expensive equipment:

To view digital teaching portfolios, a person must know how to access digital information on a CD or the Web and a computer. Whereas all principals, employers, teacher educators, and parents can view the contents of a traditional portfolio in a notebook only those with access to a computer and "know-how" can view digital teaching portfolios.

6. The presentation of information in digital format can often detract from content:

The same technology that highlights a teacher's professional competence can obstruct the view if it not used properly. High-tech "bells and whistles," might distract the viewer from important content a portfolio contains.

CHAPTER 2: SOME BENEFITS OF DIGITAL TEACHING PORTFOLIOS

It is ironic that teachers, who focus so much time and energy on their students' growth and development, have so little time and energy to focus on their own. In this chapter we describe many of the benefits that result when teachers make time to focus on their own development through the creation of digital teaching portfolios.

Professional Benefits for Teachers

Both the processes involved in creating a portfolio and the product that results from it have value for teachers. The learning that teachers experience during the portfolio development process can often improve their self-esteem, energy level, and enthusiasm. This learning process can lead to improved working conditions, more healthy classroom environments, and an increased understanding of the various aspects of professionalism if the portfolio process is structured properly. The product of learning demonstrated in a portfolio is also valuable when it communicates teacher competence and professionalism to a school community. Here we describe just a few personal and professional gains derived from digital teaching portfolios and the processes that go into creating them.

Creation of Digital Teaching Portfolios Makes Teachers Learners

Perhaps the most compelling reason for involving teachers in creating digital teaching portfolios is overlooked in the literature on portfolios. Surprisingly few "portfolio advocates" recognize that something wonderful occurs when teachers create digital

10

teaching portfolios—they get the chance to become learners. When creating their digital teaching portfolios, teachers learn about themselves (everyone's favorite topic), their profession, and new technologies. But most importantly they experience anew what it feels like to be a learner. They are reintroduced to the dilemmas and delights of the learning process. What better experience could there be to increase teachers' empathy with their students!

Teachers, like most adults, rarely have the opportunity to put themselves in environments where they are totally immersed as learners—exposed to totally new vocabulary, concepts, and conventions. Plainly speaking, environments where adults' prior knowledge becomes useless are hard to find. Plunging into the learner's environment can provide teachers important new insights and old understandings long forgotten making them better teachers.

Digital Teaching Portfolios Provide Teachers Opportunities to Learn about Technology

The creation of digital portfolios can act as a catalyst for teacher development in many professional areas but especially that of technology. During the production process, teachers have legitimate reasons to use technology equipment in meaningful ways. They have motivation to experiment with different types of hardware (i.e., computers, digital cameras, scanners, video cameras) and software (i.e., image creation and manipulation software, web editing software) and develop new knowledge and skills. By creating digital portfolios, teachers put their knowledge and learning to the test by combining technology skills with their professional knowledge to create a tangible product. In addition, the creation of a digital teaching portfolio allows them to become fluent in various areas addressed by technology standards, such as those that have been developed by the International Society for Technology in Education (2000).

11

Digital Teaching Portfolios Enhance Teachers' Impact on Students

Although the notion that a student's use of technology improves his or her learning is long on anecdotal evidence and short on hard data, we believe teachers' experiences with technology, such as what they gain in the digital portfolio process, can improve student learning in several ways. At the very least, teachers who create their own digital teaching portfolios are aware of the potential that technology has for enabling the creative process. Having had the opportunity to demonstrate their own knowledge with a variety of media, they understand the value of representing learning and growth in the well-rounded ways that digital media enables. Teachers who have seen how their own skills and knowledge can be demonstrated in various mediums are more likely to provide their students this opportunity. Teachers might offer their students the chance to create digital learning portfolios or simply look for multiple indicators of learning as a result of a satisfying experience doing so themselves. At the very most, the technical skills that teachers develop by creating a digital teaching portfolio can be put to use to improve teaching and learning. Teachers who use multimedia to create materials can help students by presenting information in more efficient, effective, and engaging ways.

Digital Teaching Portfolios are Effective Tools for Demonstrating Teacher Competence

Portfolios are a powerful way for teachers to demonstrate their professional competence to others. Whether the "others" include prospective employers, school parents, or state certification officers, the artifacts included in teachers' portfolios can speak volumes about their proficiency in areas such as curriculum planning, instruction, home-school communication, and professional knowledge. After all, what better way to "show your stuff" than to actually show your stuff!

Many states now require teachers to submit portfolios for initial and advanced certification. Methods of assessing portfolios are being developed that promise to provide those interested in measuring teacher quality with an alternative. And perhaps this method will be superior to that of using student performance on standardized tests. In a time when credibility of and respect for educators is diminishing, the promotion of information about teacher quality is of great importance. Teachers' professional competence and expertise need to be displayed for all to see. Digital teaching portfolios can be shared with the community, parents, and colleagues online in relatively convenient and inexpensive ways.

Digital Teaching Portfolios Help Teachers Get Jobs

The trend of dragging weighty binders and notebooks along to job interviews has been growing in popularity since the late 80's. But in these days of personal data assistants and laptop computers, heavy, oversized reference items no longer guarantee teachers the "edge" they did in the past. Merely having a teaching portfolio is not good enough any more. Despite the "teacher shortage" and proliferation of teaching positions in some United States regions, when teachers compete for prized jobs, every advantage counts.

Today's employers are looking for technologically savvy teachers. Even when teachers create the most simple of digital portfolios, the fact that their credentials appear in multimedia format communicates their willingness to innovate, their interest in developing new skills, and their effort to appear professional. For teachers who are highly skilled and technologically sophisticated, digital portfolios offer the only way for them to showcase the instructional materials they have created with technology. After all, you cannot demonstrate multimedia quite as effectively with a pencil and paper.

Digital Teaching Portfolios are More Portable

Digital teaching portfolios are more practical and convenient than traditional portfolios for several reasons. First, they are lightweight and easy to carry. With them, teachers who are interviewing can post-pone toting their large over-sized canvas bags until after they get a teaching job! Second, digital teaching portfolios preserve precious, often irreplaceable, primary-source materials. Let us face it, if students' lunch money is not secure in schools, neither is a teacher's portfolio. In the past, when job candidates wanted to provide school administrators time to review their credentials, they left the only original copy at the school for a while because there was no alternative. Now there is no reason. Using digital technology to create a teaching portfolio makes it possible to scan copies of artifacts. By doing this, not only are these artifacts safer but they are more accessible as well! Multiple copies of portfolios in digital format can be burned on CD-ROM and reproduced inexpensively or presented on the web and disseminated widely.

There is still a place for portfolios produced in traditional formats. But we suggest that this place is in teachers' classrooms where students and visiting parents can review their teachers' accomplishments in hard copy format (in sheet protectors of course!). In classrooms where students are encouraged to create portfolios, a teacher's portfolio carries more than a message about the teacher's competence. The mere presence of a teacher's portfolio acts as an endorsement for students' participation in this vital learning experience. After teachers are finished making digital copies of the hard evidence in their portfolios, this work should take a place of honor in the classroom.

Portfolios are a Tool for Charting Future Professional Growth

Digital teaching portfolios also can act as springboards for future professional development in several ways. First, such portfolios are biographical in that they provide a snapshot of a teacher's competence in a certain period of time. By creating and examining a biographical portfolio, teachers can reflect upon what they have accomplished, what they are accomplishing, and what they still wish to accomplish. Along these lines, teachers can also reexamine their beliefs and philosophies to see how they have grown professionally and philosophically. Second, teachers can create a digital portfolio that includes a plan for professional development—and as time progresses, teachers can refer to the portfolio to see if they have stayed on course. Third, by examining portfolios both teachers and other personnel (such as the principal) can help determine what the teachers' needs for more professional growth are and how to achieve them. For example, a teacher might have a great deal of supporting data for several standards, but not much for one of them. The standard that has not been adequately addressed in the portfolio may be an area in which the teacher might want to invest some time.

Personal Benefits for Teachers

Separating the personal and professional dimensions of teaching can be quite difficult. Many good teachers make no division between these dimensions. Perhaps this is one reason that being a good teacher is so exhausting! And yet, when discussing the benefits of digital teaching portfolios, we believe it worth mentioning that there are benefits that influence a person's well-being and happiness separate from his or her role as a teacher.

15

examine beliefs and philosophies

Portfolios Promote a Sense of Accomplishment and Satisfaction

Many teachers experience a great deal of satisfaction with their work (they must, otherwise, why would they work so hard for so little pay?). Creating a digital teaching portfolio results in a tangible product that illustrates the bulk of their work in one place. Reflecting upon their work during and after the creation process can remind teachers of their accomplishments and boost their job satisfaction.

Portfolios are Evidence of Personal Growth

Some parents make it a habit of recording their children's heights on a doorframe or wall in their homes periodically. Those who do are aware of the proud feelings their children experience when looking over the successive marks recording their physical growth. Portfolios, for many teachers, become equally effective ways to measure professional growth. Teaching portfolios created in digital format, because their storage space is almost infinite, have the advantage of recording even more benchmarks for teachers. They demonstrate growth data over a long period of time and can be an even greater cause of satisfaction.

Skills Learned to Create Portfolios Have Personal Applications

Many teachers we know have put the skills they developed when creating digital teaching portfolios to work for personal reasons. What better proof could there be that the technical skills many teachers gain during the portfolio process are enjoyable, fun, and useful! One fourth-grade teacher who learned how to put her work onto the Internet created a website for a friend's wedding. Not only did she save money on a wedding gift—she made it possible for the bride and her family to share important travel information with their guests! Another teacher created a multimedia CD displaying her family's history along with family photos, videos, and sound files. Her family was delighted when she distributed her high-tech creation as a holiday present.

In many cases, teachers devote more time applying the skills they learn for personal than professional use. Maybe this is due to the fact that people are often more invested in personal projects than professional ones. Or perhaps it is due to the fact that personal projects rarely have stringent deadlines and other time constraints. Regardless, the skills acquired during personal experimentation result in greater skill that can be applied for productive reasons in both personal and professional dimensions.

Teachers with whom we have worked have proven their skills are financially, as well as personally valuable. Some have secured summer and part-time work doing multimedia development and web design for small businesses such as real estate offices and travel agencies. Others have found the digital teaching portfolio process life-altering. These teachers discovered new talents and interests when developing their digital portfolios and ended up pursuing advanced degrees in instructional design and technology-related fields.

CHAPTER 3: THE DIGITAL TEACHING PORTFOLIO PROCESS

There is no one right way to create a portfolio just the same as there is no one right way to blend and age a critically acclaimed wine. But, our experiences with both have taught us that more and less effective approaches exist!

There are five basic stages in the development of a portfolio. Each of these stages consists of several distinct processes or steps. The five basic stages of the digital teaching portfolio process are:

- Planning the portfolio—In this stage, you focus the goals of your portfolio and frame its objectives.
- Considering portfolio contents—In this stage, you collect, select, and reflect on the materials you will include in your portfolio.
- Designing the portfolio—In this stage, you organize the materials you have selected and assemble them into digital pieces that make up your portfolio.
- Evaluating the portfolio—In this stage, you conduct formative evaluation to improve your portfolio-in-progress and summative evaluation to determine the quality of your portfolio in toto.
- Publishing the portfolio—In this stage, you perform the activities necessary to present your portfolio materials in a format that others can view.

Stage 1: Planning your portfolio

The first stage of the portfolio development process involves two different processes that will help you plan your

ge 1 focusing fitting

portfolio. In this stage, you will make decisions about the purpose of your portfolio and its intended audience. We call this process "focusing." When planning, you also will make decisions that will help you create continuity among the various components of your portfolio. Because this process involves fitting various pieces together, we call it "framing."

Focusing Your Portfolio: Defining the Purpose and Audience

When focusing your portfolio, you identify the purpose(s) for and the intended audience of your portfolio. Decisions you make at this stage dramatically influence work at all the stages and steps that follow. With so many good reasons for creating a portfolio you may wonder where to start. Start by examining your objectives for creating a portfolio in the first place. Are you creating a portfolio to get a job or to keep one? Are you creating it to earn or renew your teaching certification? Are you creating it to demonstrate or model the portfolio process for your students? Maybe you are just creating a portfolio for fun or to help yourself organize your professional credentials.

Regardless of your motivation, conscious awareness of it will help you consider the intended audience which in turn can enable you to design a portfolio that is more "in tune" with its concerns. There are many groups for whom you might create your portfolio and most likely more than one group will view it. However, it helps to have one target group in mind whether it be other teachers, your students, administrators, teacher education professors, or state certification officers.

To help your define the purpose and audience of your portfolio, answer the following questions:

1. Why am I creating this portfolio in the first place?

2. What kind of portfolio do I want to create (working, presentation)?
3. Who am I creating the portfolio for (principal, professor, me, licensure board)?
4. What are my goals (short- and long-term) for creating a digital teaching portfolio?

Framing Your Portfolio

When you frame your portfolio, you set up structures that fit various pieces together—creating continuity among the various components. Continuity in a portfolio might be communicated through a theme or set of recurring ideas, values, or metaphors. It may also be created by centering your professional growth on the investigation of a self-exploratory question or set of professional standards.

Framing Your Portfolio Around a Theme

Some teachers believe that using a theme as the central connection among the diverse artifacts contained within a portfolio promotes continuity while also illustrating their artistry as a teacher. These teachers find the organization of a portfolio expresses talent and creativity just as much as the artifacts contained within it. Themes might reflect a teacher's philosophy of education, professional concerns, or personality traits. The contents as a whole paint a vivid picture of the teacher as a creative professional.

To develop your portfolio around a theme ask yourself these questions:

1. Is there any metaphor, idea, or image that recurs in my life or sums up who I am as a teacher?
2. How could I demonstrate my professional talents by illustrating them through this theme?
3. What artifacts might I include to do this?
4. How might I use the help of others to make sure that my theme is consistent and understandable to others?

Framing Your Portfolio Around a Question

When a portfolio is developed around a question, the portfolio demonstrates the creator's ability to practice two important professional traits--introspection and reflection. First, a teacher develops a compelling question of a professional nature such as, "How do I engender intrinsic motivation and life-long learning among my students?" Then all artifacts are selected to answer this question. Reflective statements, comments written by the teacher that describe his or her thoughts on the importance of the artifact in light of the question, compliment the artifacts in answering of the question. Developing a portfolio around a question demonstrates a teacher's thinking processes and professionalism.

To learn how you might develop your portfolio around a question, read Chapter 5, "Planning your portfolio," of Kilbane, C.R., & Milman, N.B. (2003). *The Digital Teaching Portfolio Handbook: A How-to Guide for Educators*. Boston: Allyn & Bacon.

Framing Your Portfolio Around a Set of Standards

Framing a portfolio around a set of standards for initial certification or recertification is required in some states. Even if it is not required, framing a portfolio around standards can help teachers examine their knowledge and skills to see how their professional practice stacks up to what educational professionals consider good teaching.

For activities that will help you develop your portfolio around a set of standards, read Chapter 5 of Kilbane, C.R., & Milman, N.B. (2003). *The Digital Teaching Portfolio Handbook: A How-to Guide for Educators*. Boston: Allyn & Bacon.

Stage 2: Considering Portfolio Materials

You begin the second stage of the portfolio development process by collecting as many resources or artifacts from your teaching as possible. Then you select a subset of artifacts from this larger collection based on some kind of criteria tied to the focus and framework of your portfolio. Finally, you reflect on how these pieces fit together to best communicate the goals of your portfolio to your intended audience.

Artifacts and Supporting Documentation

The resources you include in your portfolio can be classified into two basic categories: artifacts and what we call "supporting documentation." Artifacts are the elements critical to the focus and framing of your portfolio because they demonstrate your professional knowledge and competence. Résumés, lesson plans, educational philosophy statements, and classroom management plans are all considered tangible evidence of teachers' knowledge.

Resources that are meaningful because they communicate important information about you as a person but do not illustrate your professional knowledge and competence and resources that help your audience understand the purpose of your portfolio better are called "supporting documentation." These resources might include personal information, the rationale statement, and table of contents.

For more information about what kinds of artifacts and supporting evidence you might include, read Chapter 5, "Planning your portfolio," of Kilbane, C.R., & Milman, N.B. (2003). *The Digital Teaching Portfolio Handbook: A How-to Guide for Educators*. Boston: Allyn & Bacon.

Collecting Portfolio Content

Organization makes the process of collecting materials for possible inclusion in your portfolio less tedious and nerve wracking. First, locate as many artifacts as possible. The more items you have to choose from, the more choices you will have in the selection process. Every choice you make about whether or not to include an artifact will lead to your professional growth because each decision causes you to think critically about your professional competence.

Based on our work with teachers, we believe that there are certain items that every digital teaching portfolio should include. These include a rationale statement (an explanation of your goals for the portfolio) and an educational philosophy statement (a document describing your core beliefs and practices in your profession). Once you have assembled these items, save them carefully in a file folder (physical—in a filing cabinet) and in a folder (digital) on your computer with the title "portfolio" depending on the format (i.e., hard copy or digital file).

Should included in portfolio

Selecting Portfolio Content

The selection of portfolio content is an important, challenging, and rewarding part of the portfolio process. It involves

23

Think about these

many decisions regarding what kinds of resources to include, which samples of artifacts to include, and how many artifacts to include (i.e., the number of lesson plans). These decisions take a great deal of energy and thinking. Often it is helpful to seek the advice of others. Even though selecting takes a long time, the process is rewarding because it enables you to review the work you have accomplished as a teacher and encourages you to consider its merits and shortcomings.

The most appropriate artifacts are selected based on certain criteria. These criteria should relate directly to the framework of your portfolio (i.e., standards, theme, or question). For instance, if your portfolio is focused around standards, then you will develop criteria that relate to the standards. Criteria might require that artifacts: 1) reflect accomplishment of specific standards, 2) illustrate continuous instructional improvement related to standards over time, 3) communicate accomplishment of specific standards.

Although it is possible to include every single artifact you can think of in your digital teaching portfolio. It is not feasible or desirable. First, you do not want to subject your audience to more artifacts if reviewing fewer artifacts might accomplish your objectives just as effectively. Less can often be more! Second, the process that goes into selecting the best or most appropriate artifacts from a larger body of artifacts can be valuable. This process requires you to make deliberate decisions about selection based on various criteria. (i.e., Is the work my best work? Does it demonstrate growth? Does it reflect a standard?) When you compare work to certain criteria (regardless of what the criteria are) you critically consider whether artifacts stack up to the criteria or not. In many cases, this means teachers are acknowledging various significant attributes of their work and learning about their own progress. By including materials without making any decisions about them, an opportunity for important professional reflection is missed.

24

Complete the following activity to help you select the artifacts you wish to include in your digital teaching portfolio:

1. Examine as many artifacts as possible (i.e., lesson plans, student work samples, etc.)
2. Determine which artifacts support the standards, theme, or question you have chosen as the foundation of your portfolio by asking yourself the following questions about each artifact/item:

- Does this artifact/item meet the criteria for which I am framing my portfolio? How?
- Is this artifact/item the best example(s) I can use for demonstrating these criteria? If so, why? If not, why not?
- Should I include this artifact/item in my portfolio? Why? Why not?

3. Create a log sheet (See Chapter 5, "Planning your portfolio," of Kilbane, C.R., & Milman, N.B. (2003). *The Digital Teaching Portfolio Handbook: A How-to Guide for Educators*. Boston: Allyn & Bacon for an example of a log sheet.) of the artifacts you wish to include in your working portfolio (and relate these to how they meet the standards, theme, or question you have chosen as the foundation of your portfolio). You may even want to rate the items (i.e., definitely include or maybe include)
4. Be selective—you do not have to include every lesson in a unit. You can include representative lessons
5. Remain focused—Keep your purpose and audience in mind when selecting artifacts.

Reflecting on Portfolio Content

A [digital teaching] portfolio without reflection is just a multimedia presentation, or a fancy electronic résumé, or a digital scrapbook (Barrett, 2000).

Reflection should occur naturally throughout the entire portfolio development process (and beyond). But what is reflection? Lyons (1998) defines reflection as "a drawing together of long strands of connections, the weaving together of experiences, theory, and practices into meaning for the individual teacher and a kind of construction of knowledge—a knowledge of teaching practice" (p. 106). We like to describe reflection as taking time to think and contemplate metacognitively about teaching practice.

Complete the following activity to help you reflect on the artifacts you have chosen to include in your digital teaching portfolio:

Ask yourself these questions about each artifact:

1. How does this artifact demonstrate competence in a particular standard (or your chosen framework)?
2. Why did I include this artifact (why is it important to me)?
3. What did I learn as a result of using/creating this artifact?
4. How would I do things differently as a result of the artifact?

Writing Reflective Statements

There are several ways that you can write and organize reflective statements. You can use the questions listed above or follow guidelines that you or others have developed. Some teachers like to include reflective statements for each artifact, whereas others like to include reflections on portions of their portfolio. For National Board Certification, NBPTS (2001) requires teachers to describe, analyze, and reflect on each artifact they include in their portfolios.

Brown and Irby (2001) recommend the use of a specific process for structuring and developing reflective comments. The process involves five steps. These are:

1. Select the artifact
2. Describe the circumstances (who, what, where, when) surrounding the artifact
3. Analyze why you chose this artifact and how it demonstrates competence/knowledge of particular standards
4. Appraise the artifact by examining and interpreting the "impact and appropriateness" (p. 32) of teacher actions and how these relate to professional knowledge
5. Transform – describe how the artifact can promote changes or growth that might improve teaching practice

Read Chapter 6, "Considering Portfolio materials," of Kilbane, C.R., & Milman, N.B. (2003). *The Digital Teaching Portfolio Handbook: A How-to Guide for Educators*. Boston: Allyn & Bacon to learn more about how you might reflect on your artifacts.

Stage 3: Designing the Portfolio

Organizing and Producing the Portfolio

The design stage involves two distinct processes that are interrelated—organizing and producing. Organizing involves: 1) the creation of a table of contents, 2) putting artifacts into the different categories found in the table of contents, and 3) the development of a storyboard that sketches out how artifacts will

27

appear to the viewer. Producing is the transformation that occurs when the storyboard and table of contents become a collection of integrated digital files. Activities in Chapter 7, "Designing the Portfolio: Organizing and Producing the Portfolio," Kilbane, C.R., & Milman, N.B. (2003). *The Digital Teaching Portfolio Handbook: A How-to Guide for Educators*. Boston: Allyn & Bacon will help teachers to complete each of these processes.

Organizing the Portfolio Contents through a Table of Contents

An excellent way to start organizing the elements of your portfolio is to create a table of contents. The table of contents represents the categories in which you will group the different items that will make up the portfolio. It also will serve as your "navigation scheme" linking the different parts of your digital teaching portfolio. Read Chapter 7, "Designing the Portfolio: Organizing and Producing the Portfolio," of Kilbane, C.R., & Milman, N.B. (2003). *The Digital Teaching Portfolio Handbook: A How-to Guide for Educators*. Boston: Allyn & Bacon to learn about ways you develop your table of contents.

Putting Artifacts into Different Categories

Once you have developed the table of contents, you will be ready to begin grouping artifacts and supporting documentation into the different categories. You will need to classify the items you chose in the selection process into the specific categories that were developed in the activity for developing a table of contents in Chapter 7, "Designing the Portfolio: Organizing and Producing the Portfolio," from of Kilbane, C.R., & Milman, N.B. (2003). *The Digital Teaching Portfolio Handbook: A How-to Guide for Educators*. Boston: Allyn & Bacon.

You can sort the items into categories using index cards or sticky notes. If these low-tech options do not appeal to you, feel free to take advantage of the graphic or outlining features in Microsoft's products or in a concept-mapping program like Inspiration and Kidspiration. We like to use Inspiration and Kidspiration because they are simple and have many different applications. A 30-day trial version of both software programs is available for free at http://www.inspiration.com. For more information about organizing the items of your portfolio, read Chapter 7, "Designing the Portfolio: Organizing and Producing the Portfolio," of Kilbane, C.R., & Milman, N.B. (2003). *The Digital Teaching Portfolio Handbook: A How-to Guide for Educators.* Boston: Allyn & Bacon

Whichever option you choose, the end result will be a comprehensive list of the contents of each category in the table of contents. We recommend creating the categories and the contents of each in digital format, as it will be easy to convert into a helpful navigational tool at later points in the design phase.

Storyboarding

Once you have developed your table of contents, you are ready to begin creating the storyboard. The storyboard is a visual plan or sketch of your portfolio. The process of creating a storyboard will force you to think about how you plan on presenting information in your portfolio. The storyboard itself demonstrates the layout of the different pieces or "nodes" of information in your portfolio. It also maps out your expectation of how viewers will move or "navigate" through various parts of the portfolio.

Information presented in digital format has the capability of being presented in two different styles—linear and non-linear. See

Figure 7-3, "Linear Design Structure," from Kilbane, C.R., & Milman, N.B. (2003). *The Digital Teaching Portfolio Handbook: A How-to Guide for Educators*. Boston: Allyn & Bacon for an example of a linear design structure. In this example, viewers must move from one page or slide to the next—but cannot move to a particular page or slide if they want.

We recommend that you create a portfolio that uses a non-linear navigation style. This style, one most of us are familiar with from our interactions with web pages on the Internet, enables viewers to select from multiple entry points to the data in your portfolio. It also allows viewers to determine for themselves which navigational paths they will follow through the information in your portfolio (linear navigation styles only enable viewers to navigate information in one way—the way the designer wants them to view it). Given their freedom to determine navigation, your viewers will go directly where they want to find specific information about you.

If you develop your portfolio with a non-linear navigation style, you might choose from several different structures for the information. The most popular are the branching and star styles (see Figure 7-4, "Non-linear Design Structures," from Kilbane, C.R., & Milman, N.B. (2003). *The Digital Teaching Portfolio Handbook: A How-to Guide for Educators*. Boston: Allyn & Bacon) although many other non-linear styles exist. The selection of different styles may be based on the amount of information you have and your skills as a multimedia designer.

If you followed our instructions for organizing your resources by creating categories for a table of contents and deciding on the contents of each category, storyboarding will be an easy task. Complete Activity 7-3, "Creating a Storyboard," from Kilbane, C.R., & Milman, N.B. (2003). *The Digital Teaching Portfolio Handbook: A How-to Guide for Educators*. Boston: Allyn & Bacon, to create the storyboard of your digital teaching portfolio using paper and pencil. Or, use the same general strategies in the activity to create your storyboard using Inspiration (or another software program with which you feel comfortable).

It is important to note that both the table of contents and the storyboard are merely planning tools that can and probably will be changed as you progress through the portfolio development process.

Things to Consider Before Producing Your Portfolio

Once you have developed a table of contents and the storyboard for your portfolio, you will be ready to transform this plan into a compilation of digital files provided you have already taken care of several things. At some point, and (if not before then definitely now!) you will have to make a decision about the software you will use to put materials together. Chapter 11, "Selecting Software For the creation of your digital teaching portfolio" of Kilbane, C.R., & Milman, N.B. (2003). *The Digital Teaching Portfolio Handbook: A How-to Guide for Educators.* Boston: Allyn & Bacon has useful information that you should consider before selecting the software program(s) to use. Various factors will serve as the basis for your choice including your skill level, access to software, the capability of your software equipment, and the storage medium you will use to share your portfolio materials.

Second, you will want to make sure that all of your materials are in the appropriate digital format that is compatible with the software program you are using to develop your portfolio. You may need to convert materials into digital format if they were not created using a computer. If materials were created in a digital format and they are not compatible with the software program you have selected, you will need to convert them to files that are compatible. Third, you will want determine which resources will be most necessary for your work and have made provisions to access them. The resources you might need range from a simple computer and software program, to other more advanced equipment, to people who might help you develop the portfolio. The software with which you choose to create your portfolio will determine your hardware, software, and personnel needs.

Producing Your Portfolio

Regardless of the software program you are using, there will come a point in the production process when each of the materials in your portfolio (each one represented by the categories in the table of contents) will become either one part of a larger digital file making up your portfolio, or one file in a collection of files that make up your portfolio.

Several strategies exist for creating digital files. Not all will save you time and promote consistency in the graphic design of every page or slide of your portfolio. Because each software program works differently, we present a strategy that will work with most programs for producing a digital teaching portfolio: the creation of a template file. Creating a template file consists of several steps: 1) the creation of a "master" or "template" file that has settings for all the graphic elements of a page or slide which is the pre-set or "model" page or slide for the portfolio, 2) the testing of the template file to determine whether all of its features work, 3) the creation of each new file from the master template file, and 4) the saving of each new file with a new name. Complete Activity 7-4, "Creating a Template for your Digital Teaching Portfolio," from Kilbane, C.R., & Milman, N.B. (2003). *The Digital Teaching Portfolio Handbook: A How-to Guide for Educators*. Boston: Allyn & Bacon, to create a template using the software program you have chosen for creating your digital teaching portfolio (i.e., Composer or PowerPoint).

Stage 4: Evaluating the portfolio

In recent years, the word "evaluation" has developed a bad connotation among teachers. But evaluation is not a four-letter word and does not have to be one! Evaluation is an important part of the development of any instructional material. Whether you have considered it or not, your portfolio is an instructional material. It may even be one of the most important instructional materials you will create! Your digital teaching portfolio serves to teach others about your professional competence. Because you are a teacher, the ease, speed, and depth with which your portfolio teaches others about your capabilities is as important an indication of your competence as the actual artifacts in it.

Two Kinds of Evaluation

There are two kinds of evaluation: formative evaluation and summative evaluation. Both methods of evaluation play important roles in the portfolio development process. Help from others is essential to make both types of evaluation useful because designers are usually not able to be constructively critical of their own work.

Formative evaluation is evaluation that occurs during the development of instructional materials. The focus of formative evaluation is to determine whether the materials (in this case the portfolio) fulfil the intended purpose. Central to formative evaluation is the purpose or goals of the portfolio. It is pretty difficult to evaluate a portfolio if no purpose exists. To understand formative evaluation, imagine a chef tasting soup while she is cooking it. Because the soup is still in its formative stage, the chef can change the recipe as needed to improve the soup.

Summative evaluation happens after an instructional material has been created. The focus of this evaluation is to determine the quality of the instructional materials (the portfolio). Quality is usually measured by how well something compares with a certain set of standards. To understand summative evaluation, imagine a crowd at a dinner party tasting and deciding how well they like the soup the chef has made. At this point, it is too late for the chef to improve the soup. It is left up to the crowd to decide upon its quality. They each have ideas about the soup's quality. Each will decide how well the soup stacks up to their idea of what soup should taste like, look like, and smell like. Then, sometimes the crowd will make a judgment about how good the chef is based on her soup.

Formative Evaluation of Your Portfolio

Any time you ask friends, colleagues, students, or any other people you know for input on the your portfolio while it is during one of the development stages, you are conducting an informal, formative evaluation. If you take time to carefully formulate the questions you ask these helpful individuals, you will raise the level of your evaluation to a more formal level.

You also will want to investigate the portfolio for its ability to present ideas well through graphic design, its technical requirements (is it viewable on various machines, does it cause crashes, is it possible to view easily), its cultural sensitivity (does it portray different cultures or gender appropriately), and its ability to communicate the personality of the teacher.

To help you conduct a formative evaluation of your portfolio we encourage you to find at least one critical friend. A critical friend is someone you trust that will provide you with honest and constructive criticism of your portfolio. This friend should also, be willing to listen to your needs, answer your questions, and direct you to where you can find more help. In our experience critical friends have been our peers, principals, professors, significant others, even our very own parents. For some, critical friends have been involved in the process from the get-go, and others at the very end (it just depends on when you might want to involve your critical friend and the amount of time you each have). For more information about how to do formative and summative evaluations, read Chapter 8, "Evaluating the Portfolio," of Kilbane, C.R., & Milman, N.B. (2003). *The Digital Teaching Portfolio Handbook: A How-to Guide for Educators.* Boston: Allyn & Bacon

Summative Evaluation of Your Portfolio

Although many people will examine teachers' portfolios to make judgments about how competent their teaching is, the evaluation of a portfolio really only tells you about the portfolio itself. Although it is possible to make generalizations about someone's teaching competence based on his or her performance as it is demonstrated in a portfolio, one can not really know about a person's teaching competence without actually witnessing and experiencing it.

In considering how a portfolio should be evaluated in a summative way, a rubric might be used. This would measure how well someone performed the steps and how complete their communication of various documents is. The rubric might measure:

- growth (start to finish of portfolio)
- attainment of standards (either those intended by the Might measure the effort the designer applied)
- technology skills incorporated into the design of the portfolio or those not incorporated

- both the process (in retrospect to see what the teacher gained from it), and
- the product as it relates to the steps.

Revising Your Portfolio

Revision is an ongoing part of the portfolio development process. This too can occur throughout the portfolio development process. In fact, because we like to consider digital teaching portfolios (yes, even though they are presentation portfolios!) as works-in-progress (aren't teachers always developing and growing?), we believe teaching portfolios can always use a little tinkering and improvement. After you have asked your critical friend(s) to review your portfolio, reflect upon your friend(s)' comments and suggestions, and make any necessary changes.

Stage 5: Publishing the Portfolio

Although you will benefit from the process of simply creating your portfolio and evaluating it, you will experience even greater benefits if you share the portfolio you have created with others. Publishing your portfolio enables you to communicate your professional information to others. There are various options you have for publishing and sharing your work.

Options for publishing your portfolio

Each option available for portfolio publication will make its contents available to your audience in different ways. These options include:

- Using a procedure called File Transfer Protocol

36

(FTP) to copy it to a server making it accessible on the World Wide Web. This option will make your portfolio accessible to anyone who has an Internet Service Provider and a Web browser

- Saving the portfolio on a storage device such as a CD, DVD, or Zip disk. Floppy disks could be used but generally do not have enough file storage space to contain even a small portfolio.
- Printing a hard copy of your portfolio and providing hard copies to anyone you like.

For more detailed information about publishing options for your portfolio, read Chapter 9, "Publishing the Portfolio," of Kilbane, C.R., & Milman, N.B. (2003). *The Digital Teaching Portfolio Handbook: A How-to Guide for Educators*. Boston: Allyn & Bacon.

Testing Your Site

After you have saved a copy of your entire portfolio (including any supporting files (i.e., wordprocessed, Acrobat, jpg, or gif files), then examine your entire portfolio. If you created one that can be viewed on the web, then check every single link and page to ensure that all graphics appear the way you want (on different kinds of computers) and that links are all working correctly. Also, we recommend that you review your portfolio using different platforms (i.e., Mac, PC), operating systems (i.e., Mac OS 8.1, Windows XP), versions of software (i.e., PowerPoint '97, PowerPoint 2000), and Internet browsers (i.e., Internet Explorer, Netscape Navigator) if you have created a web-based digital teaching portfolio. You may notice minor (or major) differences in the appearance of your portfolio. Finally, we close this chapter by urging you to test your digital teaching portfolio to ensure that it works and looks exactly how you like.

Why go through the trouble to test your site on different platforms, operating systems, browsers, and software versions? Well, because it is difficult to say exactly what platform, operating system, browser, and software version the people with whom you share your portfolio will use to view your portfolio. That is exactly why we recommend creating web-based digital teaching portfolios--they are accessible to practically anyone with a web browser and an internet connection!

EPILOGUE

As you create a portfolio you will embark on an important educational journey. This journey will require a great deal of energy, reflection, learning and relearning. It will make you feel both frustrated and satisfied. This journey will unite your past, present and future learning experiences. It will require you to reflect on what you have learned, make you question what you know, and push you to consider what you need to learn to grow as an educator. As you make this journey, remember that you do not have to travel alone. Although the process of creating a digital teaching portfolio is presented as one that is individual, it also can be communal. Activities need not be individual, they can be collegial. We challenge you to consider ways to share the portfolio process with others.

REFERENCES

Barrett, H. (2000). *Electronic portfolios = multimedia development + portfolio development the electronic portfolio development process.* Retrieved July 23, 2001, from http://www.electronicportfolios.com/portfolios/stage3

Brown, G., & Irby, B.J. (2001). *The principal portfolio.* 2nd Ed. Thousand Oaks, CA: Corwin Press, Inc.

International Society for Technology in Education. (2000). *Technology standards and performance indicators for teachers.* Retrieved January 29, 2003, from http://cnets.iste.org/teachstandintro.html

Kilbane, C.R., & Milman, N.B. (2003). *The Digital Teaching Portfolio Handbook: A How-to Guide for Educators.* Boston: Allyn & Bacon.

Lyons, N. (1998). Portfolios and their consequences: Developing as a reflective practitioner. In Lyons, N. (Ed.), *With portfolio in hand: Validating the new teacher professionalism* (pp. 23-37). New York: Teachers College Press.

National Board for Professional Teaching Standards. (2001). *NBPTS 2001-2003 candidate resource center.* Retrieved January 29, 2003, from http://www.nbpts.org/candidates/ 2001_02/portfolio/index.html

Shulman, L. (1998). Teacher portfolios: A theoretical activity. In Lyons, N. (Ed.), *With portfolio in hand: Validating the new teacher professionalism* (pp. 23-37). New York: Teachers College Press.

APPENDIX

TABLE OF CONTENTS FROM KILBANE, C.R., & MILMAN, N.B. (2003). *THE DIGITAL TEACHING PORTFOLIO HANDBOOK: A HOW-TO GUIDE FOR EDUCATORS*. BOSTON: ALLYN & BACON.

Chapter Four: The Benefits of Digital Portfolios for Principals, School Districts, and Schools of Education

Benefits of Digital Teaching Portfolios for Principals

Portfolios Provide Well-rounded Proof of Teacher Competence

Portfolios Demonstrate Teachers' Technical Knowledge and Skill

Benefits for School Districts

School Districts Benefit When Teachers Experience the Power of Portfolio Development

School Districts Benefit When Teachers Understand the Role of Portfolios in Authentic Assessment

School Districts Benefit When Teachers Develop Technical Skills from Creating Portfolios

School Districts Benefit When Teachers Learn to Chart Their Own Professional Growth with Portfolios

Benefits for Teacher Education Programs

Portfolios Help Schools of Education Deal with Issues of Accountability

Portfolios Promote Continuity throughout Teacher Preparation Programs

Portfolios Help Build Community in Teacher Preparation Programs

Summary

Check Your Understanding

44

NOTES

Theme - if you take away
the stress and fear of
writing by having student
write their papers in the
classroom in part one -2
paragraph at a time,
_ Workshoping as you go
_ Providing immediate feedback

_ Student working to help
each other

Then they can succeed at it.

- Simplifying the process
- Immediate feedback
- Multiple Ongoing Workshop (Immediate)

- Cooperate learning
students work to help each
other during the process

Educational Philosophy

Core belief & practices in profession

NOTES

1. I believe ~~that~~ learning any major mental disability that all students can learn, ~~Maybe~~ the pace might be different for ~~the~~ each ~~individual~~ but learning can and will occur.

2. Rational Statement (goal for portfolio)

I hope that my strategy will
- Show that students who are identified ~~as~~ in the educational system as stigmatized as failures prone to failures ~~unknown~~ for economical racial or other standard can write and will write and be successful at it if

① The fear of the subject is reduced by several factors
   ① Simplifying the process
   ② Giving Immediate feedback
   ③ Ongoing Workshp in

Classroom **NOTES** Pactice cooperative cooplearning

(4) Students work together during the process. They are allowed to help each other.

Now

* Can be done in any writing class

* Students can work at writing complete sentences one at a time if time is limited then put them together in a paragraph

* The key is to built as you go. That is if you decide that you will start with a four sentence paragraph by the end students should be writing 6-8 sentences.

Assess Learning

NOTES

Assess students progress by setting
aside time to give impromptu
writing assignment. Then evaluate

- Are students able to write
  proper sentences using
  transitional words / phrases
  to combine them
  fluidly ~~forming~~ one
  paragraph

- Are ~~the~~ three elements
  of the paragraph present.
  <u>each</u>

In the beginning students
should be able to make all the
mistakes in the world, but
should find these mistakes
lessen as the semester progressed

NOTES

NOTES

NOTES

NOTES

NOTES

718-765-2500

Maimonides

-140.00
250.00